# Types of Maps

## KEVIN CUNNINGHAM

**Children's Press®**
An Imprint of Scholastic Inc.
New York  Toronto  London  Auckland  Sydney
Mexico City  New Delhi  Hong Kong
Danbury, Connecticut

**Content Consultant**
Laura McCormick, Cartographer, XNR Productions
Madison, Wisconsin

Library of Congress Cataloging-in-Publication Data

Cunningham, Kevin, 1966–
  Types of maps / Kevin Cunningham.
      p. cm. — (A true book)
  Includes bibliographical references and index.
  ISBN-13: 978-0-531-26007-4 (lib. bdg.) — ISBN-13: 978-0-531-26238-2 (pbk.)
  1. Maps—Juvenile literature. I. Title.
  GA105.6.C86 2012
  526'.8—dc23                                          2012000629

All rights reserved. Published in 2013 by Children's Press, an imprint of Scholastic Inc.
Printed in Malaysia 108
SCHOLASTIC, CHILDREN'S PRESS, A TRUE BOOK™, and associated logos are trademarks and/or registered trademarks of Scholastic Inc.
1 2 3 4 5 6 7 8 9 10 R 22 21 20 19 18 17 16 15 14 13

**Front cover: cellular phone with digital map**
**Back cover: globe**

# Find the Truth!

**Everything** you are about to read is true *except* for one of the sentences on this page.

Which one is **TRUE**?

**T or F** Political maps show all the different landforms.

**T or F** Pictures taken by satellites help cartographers make maps.

Find the answers in this book.

# Contents

THE **BIG** TRUTH!

## Important Cartographers

A "Blue Marble" portrait of Earth

Google Maps was launched in early 2005.

# Northern Section
## Blue Ridge Parkway

Isolated by rugged highlands, mountain homesteads changed little from pioneer days to the twentieth century. The Pioneer Exhibit at Humpback Rocks (Mile 5.8) represents a typical mountain farm.

George Washington's plan for a transmountain canal was partially achieved in the mid 1800s. A short trail from the James River overlook (Mile 63.6) leads to a restored Kanawha Canal lock.

Abundant water and steep slopes create spectacular scenery in these mountains. Fallingwater Cascades (Mile 83.1) is accessible via a 1.3 mile loop trail.

6

# CHAPTER 1

# The Story of Maps

Most of us think of a map as a drawing that shows a particular place. Maybe that place is as small as a school, and we use the map to find our way around. The place may be as large as a continent. We even have maps of Mars. But more than anything, a map is a tool that provides information. It uses pictures to get its information across to a reader.

 Public parks often put up map signs so visitors can find their way around.

# A Long History

Humans probably scraped out simple maps in the dirt long before they invented spoken language. One famous map of the world was etched onto a clay tablet in Babylon, in what we know today as the Middle East, about 2,600 years ago. European explorers made the first detailed maps of what became the United States in the 1500s. These explorers sketched details of coastlines and other features as they sailed, canoed, and walked on their journeys.

Mapmakers once decorated their maps with ships, mermaids, and sea monsters.

**Cartographers combine information from several different sources to make accurate, detailed maps.**

Today's **cartographers** do not have to venture outside. They can work from an office by studying photographs and other data collected by satellites high above the earth. Photos and data help make the maps more **accurate**. A cartographer can even use a computer to combine millions of satellite photos into one giant map. People studying online satellite maps can see the details of an entire country or, with the click of a mouse, zoom in on their own backyards.

# CHAPTER 2

# Physical Maps

Where are the world's tallest mountains? How far is the nearest desert from where you live? What will a person see on a driving trip from Atlanta to Omaha? **Physical** maps can answer such questions. These maps show the physical features of the surface of the earth. A road map is one of the most used kinds of physical maps.

 Hikers often use detailed topographical, or topo, maps of an area's features.

A person can measure a distance on a map, then compare it to the map's scale to find the real distance.

## On the Road

Road maps existed centuries ago. One of the oldest is a 3,100-year-old road map from Egypt. Road maps show man-made physical features such as highways, railroad tracks, and towns. A map feature called a scale allows the user to compute distances. For example, on some maps 1 inch (2.54 centimeters) equals 100 miles (161 kilometers) on the ground. A trip covering 50 miles (80.47 km) on the road would look like 0.5 inches (1.27 cm) on the map.

Modern road maps use **symbols** to supply information. U.S. road maps use the symbol of a tent-shaped triangle to show a campground. An airplane symbol means an airport. A thick colored line might mark the route of interstate highways, while a thinner gray line might show where a vehicle can turn off. Someone who learns a map's symbols can pick up important information at a glance.

Some road maps show subway and bus systems. Special symbols can point out particular landmarks, such as Paris's Eiffel Tower.

# Lay of the Land

Many physical maps show **landforms** such as mountains, deserts, and lakes. Simple landform maps may use color to show features. Brown, for example, may be used for hills. Green could be used for plains. Other landform maps use symbols, such as triangles for mountains and trees for forests. A photomap, or a map made up of satellite photos, allows a map reader to see glaciers, deserts, or other landforms in their actual colors.

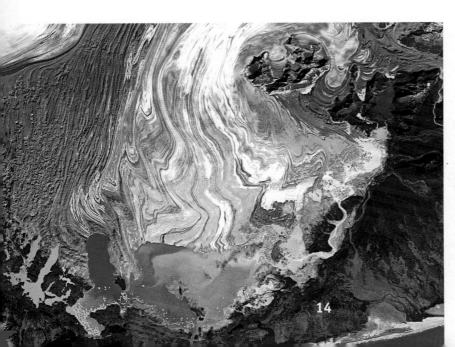

Satellite photos and photomaps provide clear views of huge landforms, such as the Bering Glacier in Alaska.

14

The first maps of the ocean were drawn by hand on sheepskin.

**A ship captain checks a chart, or ocean map, as he navigates Drake Passage near Chile.**

It takes special training to understand certain landform maps. For example, climbers read a certain kind of map to find their way into and up mountains. During wartime, a detailed map with landforms can safely guide soldiers through unfamiliar **terrain**. Maps showing physical features are necessary at sea, too. A pilot steering a ship into harbor needs to know how to avoid dangerous obstacles such as coral reefs and sandbars.

Scientists use detailed physical maps in their work. A geologist keeps maps that use color to illustrate the kinds of rocks, minerals, and fossils found in a particular area. A marine biologist uses sea maps called charts to stay on course in the ocean and underwater. Scientists also use maps to explain their work to other experts and to the public.

**Maps such as this one can help explain where an earthquake caused the most damage and why.**

# Where in the World?

The Global Positioning System (GPS) has more than 32 satellites orbiting Earth. These satellites can deliver information about location and time to a GPS receiver in any place, at any time. The U.S. Air Force operates control stations that watch the satellites, make adjustments, and keep the system working. Every day, people use GPS information in their cars, on boat trips, in the military, and in thousands of other ways.

The first GPS satellite launched in 1978.

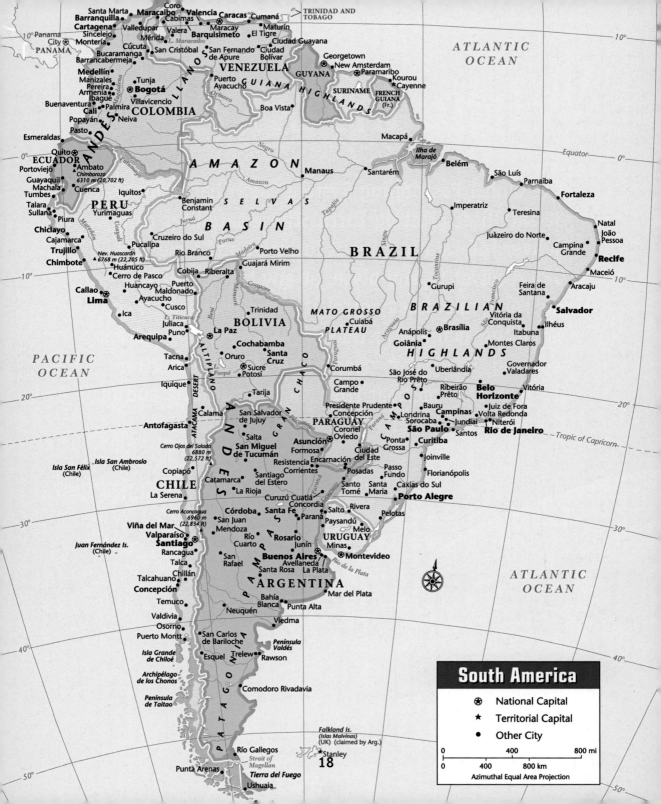

Santa Marta · Maracaibo **Valencia** Caracas Cumaná → TRINIDAD AND
Coro · · · TOBAGO
**Barranquilla** · Cabimas
**Cartagena** Valledupar · Maracay · Maturín
Sincelejo · · Valera Maracay Barquisimeto · El Tigre
Montería ⊛ Mérida · L. Maracaibo · · Ciudad Guayana
PANAMA City ⊛ Cúcuta · San Cristóbal · San Fernando Ciudad
PANAMA · Bucaramanga · · de Apure · Bolívar
· Barrancabermeja · · Georgetown
**Medellín** · **VENEZUELA** · New Amsterdam
Manizales · Puerto GUYANA Paramaribo ⊛ Kourou
Pereira · **Bogotá** · Ayacucho Orinoco SURINAME · Cayenne
Armenia · **Tunja** · · FRENCH
Ibagué · · Villavicencio GUIANA
Buenaventura · **Cali** · · GUIANA (Fr.)
· **Palmira** · **COLOMBIA** · HIGHLANDS
Popayán · · Neiva · Boa Vista
· Pasto Macapá
Esmeraldas · · · Ilha de
0° **ECUADOR** Marajó
Quito ⊛ · A M A Z O N Belém
Portoviejo · Ambato Negro Manaus · Santarém **Equator** 0°
Guayaquil · Chimborazo · · São Luís Parnaíba
Machala · 6310 m (20,702 ft) S E L V A S Imperatriz
Tumbes · Cuenca · Iquitos · · Teresina **Fortaleza**
Talara · · B A S I N Natal
Sullana · **PERU** Juàzeiro do Norte · João
· Piura Yurimaguas · · Pessoa
**Chiclayo** · Amazon Campina
Cajamarca · Cruzeiro do Sul Grande **Recife**
**Trujillo** · Pucallpa · Rio Branco Porto Velho Maceió
**Chimbote** · Nev. Huascarán · Huánuco · Guajará Mirim BRAZIL
· Callao ▲ 6768 m (22,205 ft) Cobija · Riberalta Gurupi · Feira de Aracaju
· **Lima** Cerro de Pasco · Puerto · · Santana **Salvador**
Huancayo · Maldonado BRAZILIAN Itabuna · Ilhéus
Ayacucho · · Trinidad MATO GROSSO · Brasília
· Cusco · · Cuiabá Goiânia ⊛ HIGHLANDS · Montes Claros
Arequipa · **BOLIVIA** PLATEAU · · Uberlândia Governador
· Juliaca · Cochabamba · · · Valadares
Tacna · L. Titicaca **La Paz** ⊛ · Santa Corumbá · · Vitória da
Arica · Puno Oruro · Cruz · São José do Conquista
Sucre ⊛ · Potosí Campo Rio Prêto · · Belo Vitória
Iquique · · Tarija Grande Presidente Ribeirão · Horizonte
· Calama · Prudente Prêto · Juiz de Fora
**Antofagasta** · Cerro Ojos del Salado San Salvador Concepción Bauru · Londrina **Campinas** Volta Redonda
6880 m de Jujuy · PARAGUAY Coronel Sorocaba · Jundiaí · Niterói
(22,572 ft) · Salta · Oviedo **São Paulo** **Rio de Janeiro**
Isla San Félix Isla San Ambrosio **Asunción** ⊛ · Ciudad Ponta · Santos
(Chile) (Chile) Copiapó · **San Miguel** Formosa · del Este Grossa · **Curitiba**
· de Tucumán · Resistencia Encarnación Passo · Joinville
Catamarca · · Corrientes · · Posadas Fundo
Cerro Aconcagua Santiago Santo · Santa · · Caxias do Sul Florianópolis
6960 m del Estero Tomé Maria · **Porto Alegre**
(22,834 ft) · La Rioja · Curuzú Cuatiá · Rivera
Isla San Félix **Córdoba** · Santa Fe · Salto · Pelotas
**CHILE** · San Juan · Paraná · Concordia Paysandú
Viña del Mar · Mendoza · Río · **Rosario** · Melo
**Valparaíso** · Cuarto · Junín · **URUGUAY**
**Santiago** ⊛ · San · **Buenos Aires** Minas
Rancagua · Rafael · Avellaneda Rio de la Plata **Montevideo** ⊛
Talca · Santa Rosa · La Plata
Talcahuano · Chillán · ARGENTINA · Mar del Plata
**Concepción** · Bahía
Temuco · Blanca · Punta Alta
Valdivia · Neuquén · Viedma
Osorno ·
Puerto Montt · San Carlos · Península
de Bariloche · Valdés
Isla Grande · Esquel · Trelew · Rawson
de Chiloé
Archipiélago
de los Chonos Comodoro Rivadavia
Península
de Taitao
ATLANTIC
OCEAN

PACIFIC
OCEAN

PATAGONIA

Juan Fernández Is.
(Chile)

Falkland Is.
(Islas Malvinas)
(UK) (claimed by Arg.)

Río Gallegos · ⚓ ★ Stanley
Punta Arenas · Strait of **18**
Tierra del Fuego Magellan
Ushuaia

| South America | | | |
|---|---|---|---|
| ⊛ | National Capital | | |
| ★ | Territorial Capital | | |
| • | Other City | | |

0          400          800 mi
0     400     800 km
Azimuthal Equal Area Projection

CHAPTER 3

# Political Maps

Political maps ignore most landforms. Their main
purpose is to show governmental borders and
territory. A political map often concentrates on large
areas such as countries and states. But there are also
political maps of smaller places such as counties and
school districts. A detailed political map shows capital
cities and large bodies of water. Some maps add major
towns. They might also show important nonphysical
features such as the equator or the Arctic Circle.

Brazil shares a border with
10 different countries.

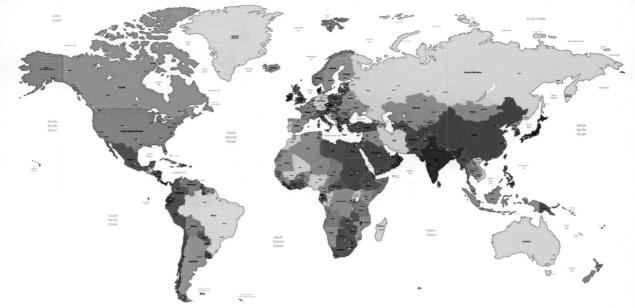

**Political maps show the borders of different countries.**

## Color the World

Cartographers usually use color to highlight different territories on a political map. That way, someone reading the map can easily see the border between, say, the United States (colored orange above) and Mexico (in red). Color also allows the reader to quickly find unconnected areas that belong to a country. For example, on the map above, the cartographer would also use orange to show Hawaii and Alaska.

## Not Quite Accurate

In the 1820s, scientist Carl Friedrich Gauss demonstrated an important problem with world maps. He proved that it is impossible to perfectly **project** the surface of a round object, such as Earth, onto a flat surface, such as paper. For that reason, cartographers must **distort** certain details when making a world map. The distortions may change the shape or size of a country.

Gauss's argument on projecting is called the *theorema egregium,* or "excellent theory."

One popular kind of world map is the Mercator map. This map makes land appear larger the farther away it is from the equator. This makes Greenland look as large as Africa. In fact, Africa is about 14 times bigger than Greenland. Cartographers may use an equal area map to solve this problem. To keep land sizes accurate and still have everything fit, an equal area map must curve the shape of the land at the map's edges.

It is impossible to map the North and South Poles on Mercator's projection. They stretch to infinity.

**A map's central point can change along with its orientation. This one has the Pacific Ocean at the center and south at the top.**

# New Kinds of Maps

Cartographers have tried to correct some of the problems with political maps. The Gall-Peters map makes each country the size it should be compared to others. The reversed, or south up, map flips the continents. This puts North America and Europe at the bottom. The new look gets people to think about how a regular world map hints that countries at the top—such as the United States and France—are more important than those farther south.

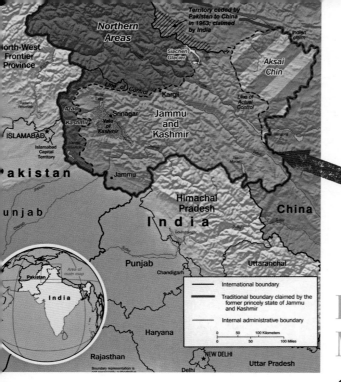

Around 12 million people live in the Kashmir region.

## Dishonest Political Maps

Governments sometimes use maps to push their point of view rather than the truth. Pakistani government maps show an area called Kashmir as part of Pakistan. But India's government maps claim Kashmir as India's. China controls small pieces of Kashmir, too. Cartographers from outside these governments try to get around the problem. Many use color or a symbol to show Kashmir as a disputed region. A note in the map's key explains which countries claim part of the area.

Some maps make places disappear. China produces maps that ignore the fact that Taiwan exists as an independent country. These maps claim Taiwan as part of China. Some maps use color, close-ups, or other methods to make one country stand out as more important. Even local maps can be dishonest. A store that seems to sit at a busy corner on an online map may actually be on a hard-to-find side street with no place to park.

Online maps do not always provide all the details you might need.

# Important Cartographers

We often do not think of maps as having authors. But some cartographers do get credit for their work. For centuries, Chinese mapmakers copied maps created by the third-century master Pei Xiu. The Blackfoot leader Ac ko mok ki made a map used by explorers Meriwether Lewis and William Clark to find their way west. A few cartographers have even become famous.

Ptolemy was born around 90 CE in Egypt. His use of a grid system and lists of where towns sat on the grid remains useful almost 2,000 years later. Ptolemy also put north at the top of his maps. The tradition continues today.

Gerardus Mercator created a new map in 1569 in an attempt to make navigation easier. Mercator's method immediately improved maps used by ships. Mercator-style maps remain popular today.

In 2000, Swiss scientist Reto Christian Stöckli led a team that used satellite images to create what became known as the "Blue Marble" pictures of Earth. The National Aeronautics and Space Administration (NASA) put out a second set of more detailed Blue Marble portraits two years later.

# CHAPTER 4

# Historical Maps

Historical maps, like other maps, provide information. But they also help people **visualize** the past. When people read an account of the 1863 Battle of Gettysburg they get a sense of what happened. But a map showing the movement of the armies on either side allows a reader to see the battle unfold. The same is true of countless other events.

 Military maps use their own symbol and color system.

# Going to the Source

A map made at the time of a historical event sheds light on what happened. Historians call such materials primary sources. During World War II (1939–1945), a cartography team drew maps of the beaches where Allied troops would invade Europe. Lieutenant William Bostick of the U.S. Navy led the team. Reading Bostick's five-color maps today gives us an idea of what soldiers faced on D-Day, the morning the invasion took place.

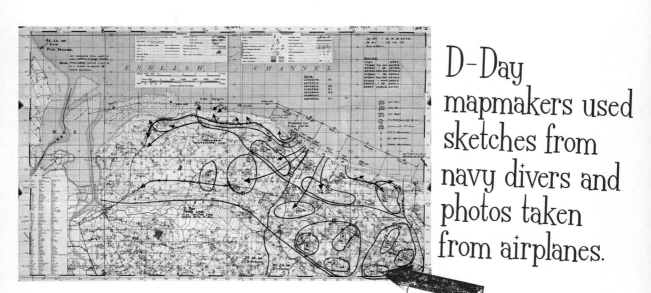

D-Day mapmakers used sketches from navy divers and photos taken from airplanes.

John Smith's map of Jamestown included drawings of the area's native people, including Pocahontas (top right corner).

# Crossing a Continent

In 1612, explorer John Smith published a map of Jamestown, Virginia. Jamestown was England's first permanent colony in what became the United States. Maps such as Smith's trace the growth of the United States from tiny colonies like Jamestown to the country of today. Historians use Smith's map to learn how well the colonists knew—or didn't know—the area. Readers can see that Jamestown was just a dot on a giant, unmapped continent.

This comparison of aerial photomaps of New York City's Battery Park shows how much the area changed between 1954 (top) and 2009 (bottom).

## Seeing Changes

Looking at a series of maps shows how things have changed. Street maps of Denver from 1880, 1920, and today reveal how and where the city grew. Take a look at the popular red and blue maps shown around election time. Southern states once always voted blue (Democrat). Now they tend to vote red (Republican). A student studying voting maps from elections over the years would know that an extreme change took place. That student might then investigate why it happened.

Maps of areas taken or bought from other countries complete the picture of the United States that is familiar to us today. A map of the Louisiana Purchase in 1803 shows just how much of today's United States was bought from France. Explorer William Clark drew maps by hand of this purchased land to provide greater detail. When put next to a map of the colonies, Clark's maps show how the United States began to come together.

Meriwether Lewis drew this map before leaving as a guide for the expedition to explore the Louisiana Purchase.

33

# Window to the Past

Historical maps also tell us what people thought about in the past. A map of the 13 U.S. colonies from 1755 shows odd borders. Virginia, the Carolinas, and Georgia stretch to the Mississippi River. At the time, people in these colonies hoped to claim the western lands. They used the map to support their claim. Today, these states stop short of the Mississippi. But the 1755 map reveals that the colonists intended to push west to control more land.

## Timeline of Important Maps

**Around 1,000 BCE**

A road map of the Egyptian Empire is made.

**Around 600 BCE**

A map of the world is created in Babylon, located in the present-day Middle East.

**1569 CE**

Gerardus Mercator produces the first map using his new method of projection.

During the Cold War (1945–1991), many Americans worried that the Soviet Union would drop nuclear bombs on the United States. During this period, there were maps showing missile bases and areas that would be least affected by bombs. Few Americans think much about these threats today. Maps marking the location of missile bases are not often produced for the public anymore. But Cold War maps show how these things once affected how Americans thought and acted.

**1612**
**John Smith's map of Virginia's Jamestown Colony is published.**

**2000**
**Reto Stöckli and his team create the "Blue Marble" image of Earth using satellite images.**

# CHAPTER 5

# Many Maps, Many Jobs

Maps are so useful, it's hard to get through the day without one. Many everyday maps fall into a category other than physical, political, or historical. But these maps also provide information. Meteorologists, for example, rely on maps. They use maps with a special set of symbols, such as a H for a high pressure system, to predict and explain the weather.

Maps that focus on a specific theme are called thematic maps.

# Mapping Climates

Some maps concentrate on the **climate** of different areas. Many popular climate maps use color. The cold Arctic is usually white. Red and orange indicate tropical warmth. Shades of green mark the temperate regions in between. Businesses might look at climate maps when deciding where to open new offices. Other climate maps help gardeners choose plants that will grow in their area. Seed packets often have a climate map broken up into colored zones on the package.

Eleven climate zones cover the United States.

Climate maps can help gardeners decide what and when to plant.

# The Cartographer's Tools

Cartographers have long used tools such as rulers and **calipers** to make their maps. But freehand drawing with paints and inks, or with sharp tools scratching into clay or bone, also played an important part in mapmaking until recent times. Hundreds of years ago, the use of a compass, quadrant, and other mechanical devices helped make the drawings more accurate. Today, hand drawing has largely been replaced by geographic information system (GIS) software and other computer-aided techniques.

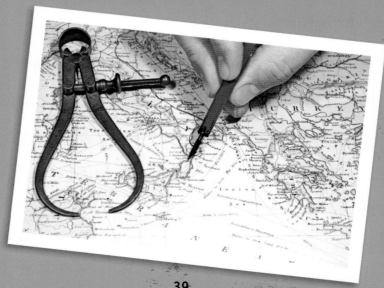

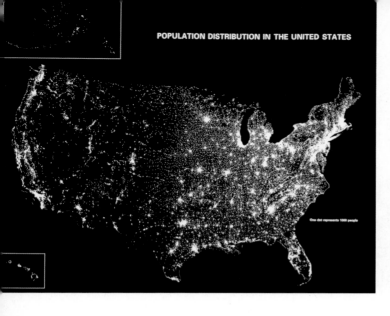

POPULATION DISTRIBUTION IN THE UNITED STATES

One dot represents 1000 people

This map shows population density in the United States. The brightest areas are where the most people live.

## People and Places

Cartographers also create **demographic** maps. These maps give information about the people in an area. Need to know how many children live in each state? A demographic map has the answer. This type of map can also show the number of flu cases in Brazil, which countries buy the most carrots, and where in the United States people say "soda" or "pop." Demographic maps have important uses in government, business, medicine, and every other field concerned with studying humans.

# Natural Resource Maps

Maps that show **natural resources** provide information on a region's products. A U.S. natural resource map may show a symbol of a gold bar in gold-mining states such as Nevada and Colorado. Apple symbols could dot Michigan and Oregon to represent orchards. A symbol for salmon might sit in the oceans off Alaska. These maps help businesses decide where to build factories. Governments can use the maps to determine what land can be logged for lumber.

**Natural resource maps help scientists keep an eye on forest resources and prevent over-logging.**

Logging was the second-deadliest job in the U.S. in 2011.

Scientists who study birds are called ornithologists.

Scientists collect data in the field in order to make wildlife maps.

## Here a Bear, There a Bear

Biologists and other scientists use maps to study living things. These maps are kind of like demographic maps for animals and plants. Experts map all kinds of information for wildlife living on land and sea. They might map flying routes of Canada geese, the number of rhinoceroses per nation, or the range of the spectacled bear. Wild plant maps track the loss of rain forests or the spread of an invasive species such as kudzu.

# Changing Maps

Maps change as technology improves. For example, pilots have started using moving maps. Information from satellites and other sources allows the maps to show the real world—landforms, buildings, and other aircraft—in real time. This way, a pilot can still "see" in thick fog or a storm or if some of the aircraft's instruments stop working. As maps continue to improve, they can save lives, help the environment, or just make it easier to get to Grandma's house! ★

**Moving maps can make flying and landing a plane at night easier and safer.**

43

Age of the Babylonian map of the world:
2,600 years old

Age of the road map from ancient Egypt:
3,100 years old

Number of satellites in the Global Positioning System: 32

Decade Carl Friedrich Gauss proved a sphere's surface could not be projected accurately onto a flat surface: 1820s

Number of Greenlands that could fit inside Africa:
About 14

Number of countries that claim parts of Kashmir: 3

Date that Mercator first drew his famous map: 1569

Date that John Smith made his map of Jamestown:
1612

Number of colors on William Bostick's D-Day maps: 5

## Did you find the truth?

(F) Political maps show all the different landforms.

(T) Pictures taken by satellites help cartographers make maps.

# Resources

## Books

Cooke, Tim, ed. *Maps and Exploration*. New York: Gareth Stevens, 2010.

Lanier, Wendy. *Maps*. Detroit, MI: Thomson Gale, 2008.

Oleksy, Walter G. *Mapping the Seas*. New York: Franklin Watts, 2002.

Oleksy, Walter G. *Mapping the World*. New York: Franklin Watts, 2002.

Walker, Robert. *Mapping Towns and Cities*. New York: Marshall Cavendish Benchmark, 2011.

**Visit this Scholastic Web site for more information on types of maps:**
★ www.factsfornow.scholastic.com
Enter the keywords **Types of Maps**

# Important Words

**accurate** (AK-yuh-rit) — correct in details

**calipers** (KAL-ih-purz) — instruments used to measure distances from point to point

**cartographers** (kahr-TAH-gruh-ferz) — scientists who make maps

**climate** (KLYE-mit) — the weather typical of a place over a long period of time

**demographic** (dem-uh-GRAF-ik) — relating to facts that come from a study about people

**distort** (di-STORT) — to twist out of the normal shape

**landforms** (LAND-formz) — features of the earth's surface

**natural resources** (NACH-ur-uhl REE-sors-ez) — materials produced by the earth that are useful to people

**physical** (FIZ-i-kuhl) — of or having to do with nature or natural objects

**project** (pruh-JEKT) — to display an image on a flat surface

**symbols** (SIM-buhlz) — designs or objects that stand for, suggest, or represent something else

**terrain** (tuh-RAYN) — an area of land

**visualize** (VIZH-oo-uh-lize) — to imagine something or see it in your mind

# Index

Page numbers in **bold** indicate illustrations

# About the Author

Kevin Cunningham has written more than 40 books on disasters, the history of disease, Native Americans, cartography, and many other topics. Cunningham lives near Chicago with his wife and their young daughter.

ML                    11-12